Through Her Eyes

Understanding Anxiety, OCD, and the Truth That You Are Not Broken

NATALIA YURECKO
WITH NANETTE YURECKO

Published by Wholeness House Press, Chanhassen, Minnesota

This book is not intended to provide medical, psychological, or mental health advice and should not be used as a substitute for professional diagnosis or treatment.

ISBN: 979-8-9950540-0-9 (Paperback)
ISBN: 979-8-9950540-1-6 (Ebook)

For every child who has wondered if they were broken
— and every parent learning how to love without fear.

Note to the Reader

This book is a story of lived experience.

What you will read here reflects our personal journey navigating anxiety, OCD, and mental health as a daughter and a mother. We share what we lived, what helped us, and what we learned along the way—not as medical or mental health professionals, but as humans finding our way through fear, healing, and growth.

Mental health is deeply personal. We recognize that no two people experience anxiety, OCD, or any mental health condition in the same way. Even the same diagnosis can look different from person to person, shaped by biology, environment, support systems, and timing.

Throughout this book, we speak from our truth—not universal truth. Some of the approaches, tools, or reflections that supported us may resonate with you; others may not. Medication, therapy, and professional care can be lifesaving and essential for many individuals, and each person's path to healing is unique.

This book is not intended to replace professional medical or mental health advice, diagnosis, or treatment. We encourage you to seek support from qualified professionals and to trust your own discernment as you navigate what healing looks like for you or your loved one.

Our hope is simple: that by sharing our story honestly, you feel less alone—and more connected to your own wholeness, strength, and capacity to heal.

How to Use This Book

This book was written for anyone whose life has been touched by anxiety or OCD—whether you are living with it yourself, loving someone who is, or learning how to walk alongside mental health challenges with greater understanding and compassion.

You do not need to read this book quickly or in order. Some readers move through one chapter at a time, allowing space for the words to settle. Others return to a single chapter when a particular season feels heavy. There is no right way to move through these pages—only the way that meets you where you are.

Each chapter explores one part of the THHRIVE framework, offering perspective, reflection, and gentle practices. These practices are invitations, not expectations. Take what resonates. Leave what does not. You are allowed to move slowly.

This book is not meant to fix you—or anyone you love. It is meant to steady you. To remind you that mental health challenges do not define who you are, and that wholeness is not something you earn. It is something you remember.

For a long time, I thought I had to get rid of my anxiety before I could really live.

If at any point you need to pause, please do. Set the book down. Take a breath. Come back when you're ready.

We hope these pages feel like a quiet companion—steady, compassionate, and reassuring—reminding you that living fully is not a destination, but a continual process of becoming.

Contents

Introduction *ix*

1: **T** – Truth: Understanding You Are Not Broken 1

2: **H** – Help: Asking for Help and Learning to Help Yourself 9

3: **H** – Health: Nourishing Mind and Body with Compassion 19

4: **R** – Radical Love: Living with Care, Honesty, and Clear Boundaries 31

5: **I** – Invest: Healing Isolation Through Connection and Contribution 43

6: **V** – Vulnerability: Releasing Guilt and Shame Through Forgiveness 53

7: **E** – Explore: Discovering Interests, Strengths, and Joy 63

8: Living the **THHRIVE** Path 73

Epilogue 77

Acknowledgments 83

About the Authors 84

Introduction

Dear God,

I pray that my family and I have a successful week with no arguing at the piano and doing well with school work.

I also pray that my whole family and I stay healthy through this rough time.

I pray that there will be sunshine, and that my mom and I can get along better.

I hope she knows that I love her.

Amen.
Thank you, God.
Natalia

I didn't know it then, but that journal entry carried the truth of everything I would come to learn. This prayer was my childhood. The reality at the time I couldn't name, but it was one me and my family lived with every day.

I believed something was wrong with me. I believed that my feelings were too much, my thoughts too loud, my fears too powerful. I tried to do everything right, to be careful, to follow the rules I felt forming inside me. I lived by these rules, and they were meant to keep everyone safe, including myself.

From the outside, I looked like a bright, capable child. Inside, my world felt intense and overwhelming. I didn't have words for it yet, only the sense that I was constantly out of place. I needed to manage myself in order to belong.

Years later, those inner rules were given a name: obsessive compulsive disorder and anxiety.

But long before the diagnosis, I had already begun asking the deeper question that lives underneath every struggle:

Am I broken—or am I human?

A Mother's Reflection

As Natalia's mother, I watched this intensity unfold from the earliest years. She was deeply curious, profoundly sensitive, and fiercely aware. By age five, a trusted friend urged us to consult a child psychologist. Testing revealed Natalia scoring in the 99th percentile across multiple measures. She was performing two years above her chronological age in all areas, which created dissonance between the cognitive and emotional maturity in her brain. We were told she would need to be challenged and also supported in learning how to "navigate her powerful responses to the world."

At the time, those words sounded hopeful.

Two years later, we returned to that same office carrying a heavier truth. The diagnosis of OCD and anxiety reshaped our everyday life. Meals, school mornings, leaving the house—ordinary moments became battlegrounds governed by fear, rituals, and invisible rules.

I believed that if I did everything right—as a mother, teacher, leader—I could fix this. I couldn't. And accepting that reality broke me open.

Yet in the breaking, something unexpected emerged.

We discovered a truth that would become our anchor:

We are not broken.

That realization didn't erase struggle. It changed how we understood it.

Through Her Eyes

This book is not a story of curing or conquering. It is a story of remembering.

It is told through two voices—a daughter learning to trust herself, and a mother learning to let go of control. Natalia's voice carries the lived experience of anxiety and OCD from the inside. My voice holds the broader arc—the witnessing, the fear, the surrender, and the love required to walk this path alongside her.

Together, we offer this story not as experts who arrived, but as humans who learned to stay.

What we discovered is simple, and radical: Pain and struggle are not evidence of failure.

They are part of the design.

There would be no healing without them.

The THHRIVE Path

From our lived experience emerged a framework we now call **THHRIVE**—seven principles that helped Natalia reclaim her sense of self and helped our family move from survival into presence, resilience, and joy.

T—Truth: Understanding you are not broken.

H—Help: Asking for help and learning to help yourself.

H—Health: Nourishing mind and body with compassion.

R—Radical Love: Living with care, honesty, and clear boundaries.

I—Invest: Healing isolation through connection and contribution.

V—Vulnerability: Releasing guilt and shame through forgiveness.

E—Explore: Discovering interests, strengths, and joy.

In each chapter, you will hear Natalia's voice—honest, searching, and grounded—alongside reflections from a mother learning to trust her child's inner wisdom. The chapters close with gentle reflections and practices—not to fix you, but to walk with you.

This is not a story of perfection. It is a story of wholeness.

And our hope is that as you read, you may begin to see, through Natalia's eyes, that you were never broken either.

1

T—Truth: Understanding You Are Not Broken

"Wholeness isn't something we earn—it's who we've always been."

Natalia

I don't remember a time without OCD.

My first memory is from preschool. My mom dropped me off, and I cried the whole morning. My stomach hurt. I refused to eat. All I wanted was for her to come back. I thought she was going to die, and I thought I was going to die. I thought something bad was going to happen. Ms. Katie came over to comfort me, "Don't worry, your mom will be back in six hours!" She probably thought I'd adjust soon, like most preschoolers. But my fear was bigger and louder than typical separation anxiety. I couldn't let my mom out of my sight and obsessed over losing her.

At five, I had my first panic attack. I had just eaten some Teddy Grahams. My stomach felt weird. I ran to the bathroom, convinced I would throw up. After I waited in front of the toilet for thirty minutes, nothing happened. I didn't know it then, but that was anxiety's first real grip on me.

Then came Christmas Eve. I woke up sick in the middle of the night. Everything changed. From then on, holidays became something to fear. I'd wake up on Christmas morning or my birthday with a pit in my stomach. Others looked forward to laughter and surprises. I braced for disaster.

At school, things got harder. Eating breakfast and lunch became a challenge. Leaving my mom was still extremely difficult. The world felt scary and uncertain.

After my OCD diagnosis, I saw the child psychologist every week for therapy. I didn't understand what that meant. My mom said it was to talk about my thoughts and feelings. But saying them out loud sounded terrifying. Speaking them made them real.

In the midst of fear and confusion, my mom's voice was the one thing that kept me going.

She'd remind me, "OCD is just a small part of your brain. It's not who you are."

That truth became my lifeline. Even when I didn't believe it, I clung to it through my uncertainty and doubt. Deep down, I wanted to believe I wasn't broken. Gradually, I noticed a shift—the more I heard it, the more hope crept in, even if I hadn't yet learned how whole I truly was.

Nanette

While other children blew out candles on their birthdays, Natalia clutched the thermometer and searched her body for signs of sickness. Holidays loomed like threats. Family traditions felt like traps. She avoided sleepovers, fled field trips, and created rituals to manage the chaos. I watched as anxiety and OCD gradually dimmed my daughter's laughter and joy, feeling powerless as fear quietly replaced her sparkle.

Little by little, OCD wove itself into our days, shaping Natalia's actions and my reactions. As her symptoms intensified and she was physically, mentally, and emotionally exhausted, one day she asked, "Mom, why is this happening to me?" Tears flooded her eyes as she looked up at me, desperately seeking an answer. Time stopped in that moment because I knew my answer would echo in her heart and mind for years. I wanted to say something wise, something that would take away the pain. But the truth was, I didn't know why. I was honest and then offered a faint adage about how in all adversity there is a seed of good.

My response brought only small comfort at first. But her question lingered, prompting deep reflection. Grappling with her pain, I recognized the shame and sadness as my own. I had lived with an eating disorder, the "sister" of OCD, in silent struggle for decades. For twenty-five years, it hid behind perfectionism and performance. Hiding it gave it power; secrecy helped it thrive. On the outside, I had the career, the degrees, the control. Inside, the eating disorder quietly destroyed my spirit, keeping me out of alignment with myself and those I loved.

When I saw fear shrinking Natalia's world, I felt a familiar dread. I knew the feeling of being trapped inside your own mind, of believing something within you was fundamentally wrong. Determined to help Natalia avoid my mistakes, I committed to changing our story. I spent time digging deep and examining my own beliefs. Through this process, I realized the real lie is believing we are broken. Our struggles do not define us; they reveal our strength and build resilience. This realization rekindled our hope and restored a sense of equilibrium.

This truth became the first principle of THHRIVE and a different approach to healing.

Truth: You are not broken. At your core, you are whole and complete. Struggles are experiences, not your identity.

Embracing this truth takes courage. It asks us to confront our flaws while still recognizing our wholeness.

Wholeness isn't about fixing. It's about remembering who we truly are, even in fear and striving.

What This Means for You

Truth is the starting point of healing. Lasting change begins by remembering our core: whole, not broken.

You are not your child's diagnosis. Your child is not their behavior. You are both more than the labels, the panic, or the pain.

When you stop seeing yourself or your child as broken, compassion, curiosity, and hope begin to emerge. You start to see progress not as perfection, but as connection.

Wholeness has always existed below fear and unwanted thoughts. Struggle reminds us to reconnect with that truth.

Youth Practices

1. **Truth Mirror**
   - Look in the mirror and say: *"I am not broken. I am brave. I am whole—exactly as I am."*
   - Repeat these phrases even when you don't believe them. Especially then.
2. **Give It a Name**
   - Choose a name for your OCD/anxiety; make it fun by giving it a silly name.
   - This helps your brain view the OCD/anxiety as something external, rather than an integral part of who you are.
3. **Safety Words**
   - Pick a word or phrase that reminds you you're okay—like "breathe," "love," or "home."
   - Whisper the word or phrase when you feel anxious. It brings your truth back online.
4. **Celebrate the Small Wins**
   - Every time you face a fear or finish a hard day, take a moment to celebrate it.
   - Wholeness isn't about falling apart—it's about showing up for yourself, again and again.

Parent/Caregiver Practices

1. **Speak Wholeness Daily**
    - Each morning, tell your child one thing that's strong, kind, or beautiful about them.
    - Example: *"I love how you keep trying, even when you're scared."*
    - Over time, this becomes their inner voice.
2. **Name the Story, Not the Identity**
    - When your child struggles, separate the behavior from who they are.
    - Example: *"OCD is tricking you right now,"* instead of "You're being difficult."
3. **Model Vulnerability**
    - Share something you're working on—without shame.
    - Example: *"Sometimes I get nervous before speaking at work, but I breathe through it."*
    - You're teaching that strength and struggle can coexist.
4. **Pause Before Fixing**
    - When your child is spiraling, resist the urge to solve the problem right away.

- Simply say, *"I'm here. You're safe. We'll get through this together."*
- Presence often heals more than answers.

Truth reminds us that healing doesn't start with fixing. It starts with remembering.

You were never broken.

You were always whole.

2

H—Help: Asking for Help and Learning to Help Yourself

"Asking for help isn't weakness—it's wisdom, the moment we remember we were never meant to heal alone."

Natalia

Perfectionism crept in early. At piano lessons, every mistake felt like failure. I'd cry and tell myself I was stupid or worthless. I couldn't bear to be less than perfect.

Then one day at a swim meet, I saw another kid throw up. I can still remember exactly which lane it happened in. I avoided that lane for years. My fear grew so big it started to rule my life.

After that, fear shaped how I approached every swim. I couldn't eat before meets and needed my mom close by, hoping it would make them easier. Before each race, my nerves caused my body to shake. Once, overwhelmed, I ran for my mom but was too late and got sick in front of everyone. I felt exposed and wanted to disappear.

My mom was angry, and now I know that anger came from fear. It was her own fear of watching me unravel under OCD. But in that moment, all I felt was lost.

For months afterward, the panic attacks continued. I barely ate. I couldn't focus in school. I lost weight, energy, and hope. The pattern repeated itself—panic, nausea, shame. By nine years old, life felt like survival. Every day was a fight between me and my thoughts.

Just making it through the school day without a panic attack, getting through swim practice without feeling sick, and eating a full meal were wins. But the stares from the other kids didn't help. I felt like an outsider. I kept to myself, zoning out, trying to stop the next panic from coming. Germs were everywhere, and so many thoughts I couldn't turn off. There was also so much my mom didn't know—the intrusive thoughts that haunted me, the rituals I used to keep myself safe, and the secret rules that ran my day.

Therapy wasn't helping. In fact, it made me feel worse. Each session ended with more frustration, more hopelessness. Instead of getting better, I felt like proof that I was beyond fixing.

Then came the meeting at PrairieCare. I barely remember

what was said, only the psychologist's calm voice saying, "I think outpatient treatment would be beneficial." Shock and guilt crashed over me. I felt the weight of making my parents rearrange their lives, take off work, and pay for more help. It all just increased my feelings of overwhelm.

Then we were off to Rogers [Behavioral Health]. I didn't know what to expect. My stomach turned, nervous and unsure, as we walked through the doors that first morning. But there, the staff greeted us with warmth. The other kids looked at me, not with pity but understanding. For the first time, I didn't feel like the only one struggling.

Rogers didn't heal me overnight, but it gave me hope. Little by little, the light came back. The therapy there was hard work, and sometimes I wanted to quit, but underneath all the fear was a quiet determination: I wanted my life back.

Slowly, I learned that asking for help made me brave.

I started telling my mom when I was scared instead of hiding it. At school, I asked for more time when I needed it. I told my swim coach that sometimes I just needed a break to breathe. Every time I asked for help, the fear got a little smaller.

And I started to notice something else. I could help myself too. Taking a breath. Using one of my coping skills. Reminding myself that I was okay. It didn't make everything easy, but it made it possible.

Help didn't mean I was weak. It reminded me we weren't alone.

And maybe that was the beginning of healing.

Nanette

Natalia began Suzuki Method piano lessons at MacPhail Center at age four. As parents were involved in this piano teaching system, I guided her daily practice after each weekly lesson.

One afternoon during practice, Natalia missed a note and slammed her hands on the keys. "I'm so stupid. I'll never get this right." Her words pierced me.

It wasn't just hearing my child speak that way. Her outburst awakened something hauntingly familiar. Her voice carried the same sharpness I had once used against myself, a language of self-punishment I knew well. Watching her crumble under that pressure felt like looking in a neglected mirror. If these were the words she spoke aloud, I could only imagine the ones she kept hidden.

That moment forced me to face a truth I had long ignored. Up until then, what I'd called *drive* or *discipline* was really *fear*—fear of not being enough, of failing, of being found out. The shift from pain to realization was jarring. I now saw I had passed that same silent fear to my daughter. It happened one practice, one sigh, one self-critical glance at a time.

Around this period, swim meets became overwhelming for Natalia. She had started swimming competitively at seven and loved the water, but over time, anticipatory anxiety stole every trace of joy. Unlike most parents who dropped their children off and returned after warm-ups, I waited in my car at her request outside for over an hour, my heart racing, just in case she needed me. Seeing her struggle through the meets and watching her burn energy while unable to eat left me feeling helpless. The OCD had ripped my heart out and then handed it back to me, overshadowing both our lives.

Therapy wasn't working either. Natalia grew defiant. She wasn't rebellious, just exhausted. Her fear masked itself as resistance. Every setback pushed us further from hope.

I felt angry at OCD for taking my only child, the daughter I'd waited and struggled for. But underneath, I was actually angry at myself.

I had begun my career as a special education teacher, working with children who had emotional and behavioral disorders, helping them believe they could weather any storm. Yet here I was, unable to help my own child. The irony was unbearable; I was standing in the downpour, holding an umbrella full of holes. All my training couldn't shield us from this.

Natalia and I were both frustrated. The weight of our struggle pressed in, clarifying that we needed help.

I knew I couldn't watch her live like this. I also knew, from my background, where to start. So I scheduled an appointment with PrairieCare—a mental health services center—for screening and support. After their evaluation, we were referred to a partial-hospitalization program at Rogers Behavioral Health, which specializes in OCD.

Help didn't come as rescue. For me, it came as relief. Allowing myself to accept help eased the burden.

It came as permission to stop pretending we could handle everything on our own.

Over the next few months, I learned that asking for help wasn't a sign of weakness. It was an act of love. It allowed us to receive care and let others into our journey, even if they couldn't solve everything.

Help, I learned, isn't a handout.

It's a hand held.

Help is not just a bridge between surviving and thriving. It is an invitation to step bravely into a life where both are possible.

What This Means for You

Asking for help is one of the bravest things you can do for yourself, and for your family. It's the moment you stop trying to carry the entire weight alone and allow love to share the load.

We are taught to admire strength, but true strength often looks like surrender: a tearful phone call, a quiet confession, a simple "I can't do this by myself."

Help does not mean weakness. It means willingness—willingness to be seen, to grow, and to believe that healing is not meant to happen in isolation.

Youth Practices

1. **Your Helper List**
   - » Write or draw three people you can go to when you're sad, scared, or worried.
   - » Keep this paper in your room or backpack so you always know who's in your corner.
2. **Help Words**
   - » Practice saying, *"Can you help me?"* in front of a mirror.
   - » Add a feeling word: *"Can you help me? I'm nervous."*
   - » Saying words out loud builds courage for the moments that matter.
3. **The Calm Jar**
   - » Fill a clear jar with glitter, water, and glue.
   - » When you're upset, shake it and watch the glitter settle. Breathe until you feel calm again.
4. **Self-Help Moments**
   - » Each night, name one time you helped yourself that day—taking a deep breath, telling the truth, asking for a hug.
   - » Whisper to yourself, *"That was brave."*

Parent/Caregiver Practices

1. **Normalize Asking for Help**
    - Share personal stories about times when seeking help made life better.
    - *"Even adults need help sometimes"* is a simple but powerful truth.
2. **Create a "Help Circle"**
    - Write down three people or resources you can reach out to when things feel heavy—a therapist, a close friend, a relative, or your faith community.
    - Keep this paper visible as a reminder that support is real and available.
3. **Pause the Perfection Script**
    - When your child struggles, replace "You'll be fine" with *"It's okay to feel scared.* Let's find someone who can help us."
    - This shifts the focus from dismissing pain to addressing it with compassion.
4. **Ask Yourself for Help Too**
    - Take one small action every day that supports your own well-being—call a friend, rest, journal, or step outside.
    - Your self-care gives your child permission to do the same.

Help is not a rescue; it's a rhythm. It's the give and take of love, the reaching and the receiving.

When you ask for help, you teach your child that healing is not something we do alone. It's something we do together.

3

H—Health: Nourishing Mind and Body with Compassion

"Wholeness grows when the mind and body remember they belong to each other."

Natalia

When I was little, I didn't think much about food. I ate when I was hungry and didn't question it. But slowly, fear took over. One day I ate something and later got sick, and my brain decided that food was dangerous.

I didn't know what ARFID was at the time. I just knew that if I ate the wrong food, or ate too much, or ate at the wrong time, I might throw up. So I started keeping track of everything. I knew what I ate, where I ate it, what time it was, and what room I was in. If something made me feel even a little nauseous once, I put it on the "Never Again" list.

Soon, the list was longer than the foods I would actually eat.

Watermelon. Swedish Fish. Pizza. Popcorn. Cheerios. Broccoli. Macaroni and cheese.

Even seeing or smelling those foods could trigger a panic attack. My brain convinced me they would make me sick again.

Breakfast and lunch weren't helping either. I told people I just wasn't hungry, but the truth was, being hungry felt safer than the possibility of getting sick. I refused to eat breakfast before school, and my untouched lunch came home. I was terrified food might make me throw up in public, so I waited to eat until I was safely back home.

Food stopped being fuel. It became fear.

Nighttime was the hardest. Like most kids, when I got a stomach bug, I'd wake up in the middle of the night to get sick. Because of that, my brain decided nighttime was dangerous. If I had eaten anything after school, panic would rise as soon as the sun went down.

What if I throw up while I'm asleep? What if I choke? What if I can't get to Mom in time?

Those thoughts kept me up until pure exhaustion finally closed my eyes. I was running on empty, and so was my mom.

I didn't understand that my body wasn't trying to betray me. It was trying to keep me safe, even if it overreacted.

At Rogers, I learned my body could do scary things and still be okay. We used exposure therapy, where I tried the foods I feared most. Slowly, I learned that it wasn't the food that caused the sickness.

They also used exposure to show me that throwing up isn't the end of the world. Some things felt silly, like making slime that looked like throw-up (I know . . . gross), but it helped. And it was really hard. There were lots of tears. Lots of "I can't do this." Lots of panic attacks.

But also lots of accomplishments.

By the end, I could stay a whole day at Rogers without my mom.

I could eat all the foods I had avoided.

I could eat **three whole meals a day.**

And I wasn't nearly as afraid of throwing up anymore.

I also learned that sleep doesn't come when you force it.

It comes when your body starts to trust again.

When my mind and body finally started working together, healing began to feel possible. And that's a lesson every family deserves to hold.

Nanette

It was December 2019. After another Thanksgiving and birthday, I anxiously awaited the call from Rogers. When it finally came as I left Starbucks, I pulled over to focus.

The woman on the phone said, calmly and efficiently, that Natalia could start the following week. Then she added, "And she'll be entering through the OCD Eating Disorder Unit."

My world stopped.

I jotted down instructions mechanically while my inner voice screamed: *No. No. No.* An eating disorder was the one thing I never wanted my daughter to inherit. Rage and guilt surged through me. *They can't be right*, I thought. I called back immediately.

"Natalia doesn't have an eating disorder," I insisted. "I don't want her around kids who do." I knew what eating disorders could teach, and I didn't want her learning those painful patterns.

The woman gently explained that Natalia wasn't being treated for anorexia or bulimia. She likely had avoidant restrictive food intake disorder (ARFID), a condition linked to OCD. Kids like her avoid foods they associate with sickness. She reassured me that if it wasn't the right fit, she could be transferred to the OCD unit. Still, I thought: *They're wrong. Wrong, wrong, wrong.*

Because she was only ten, I attended Rogers with her daily. The first two weeks were difficult for me. Entering the

Eating Disorder Unit forced me to confront the residue of my own history. Two meals a day, sitting with youth who were facing similar shadows around food—I once knew this system so well; this situation made my entire being hurt in ways I wasn't prepared for. But then came the facts I couldn't ignore: Natalia's weight and BMI had dropped from the 50th to the 5th percentile.

She wasn't growing, and I knew nutrition mattered for her body and her brain. What we eat impacts brain structure, function, and mood.

Then one afternoon, while Natalia was in individual therapy, I sat in the family waiting room. A mother sat down next to me—warm, quiet, exhausted. She shared that she was one of her son's "contaminants," a feared trigger. He couldn't bear to be near her.

My heart cracked open.

Everything OCD had taken from us suddenly felt smaller. Natalia still *needed* me. She still clung to me. She still wanted me close. My own challenges felt lighter in comparison. This new perspective allowed me to begin letting go and to place trust in the process. Perspective became grounding for both of us. We began to adapt, and together, Natalia and I took our first steps toward recovery.

As weeks passed at Rogers, pieces of our lives slowly began to return. Before Rogers, it would take hours to get Natalia to sleep, and even longer on the nights before an event. I was working as a school district administrator and managing our day-to-day lives on four hours of sleep a night. Natalia was depleted too, surviving on fumes.

Rogers helped us reclaim the night.

More sleep. More energy. More ability to cope.

Through cognitive behavioral therapy (CBT) and exposure and response prevention (ERP), they taught Natalia to face her fears instead of running from them. Since one of her obsessions was the fear of something terrible happening to me, they began sending me away from the unit, thirty minutes at a time. I used that time to walk, to breathe, to pray. And every inhale felt like reclaiming a piece of myself. Every exhale released just a little more resentment and fear.

Our bodies and our minds were learning to feel safe again.

And healing, real healing, began to seep back in. This shift in our daily lives became another foundation for deeper change, guiding us beyond tasks and toward genuine connection.

Health is a relationship, not a checklist. A relationship with your breath, your body, your brain, and your hope.

The prevailing mindset used to be that the mind controls the body. But the current mentality is that it's actually a bidirectional relationship. The mind influences the body, and the body influences the mind. So when we care for the body with sleep, fuel, movement, and breath, the mind learns it is safe to heal.

And we remember that wholeness grows from the inside out.

What This Means for You

Health isn't a checklist. It's a relationship with your child's body, as well as your own. Sleep, food, movement, and breath are not the final steps of healing, but rather the **first** steps of safety.

You are not failing if your child struggles with rest or nourishment. You are not behind if fear disrupts daily routines. This is not about willpower, it's about a nervous system working overtime to feel safe. When we honor the body's needs, the mind learns it is safe to soften.

And when we give care with compassion, trust begins to return to places where fear once lived.

Every small restoration of health—one night of better sleep, one brave bite, one moment of calm—is a step toward resilience.

Youth Practices

1. **Sleep Helpers**
   - » Choose a bedtime routine your brain can count on: a favorite blanket, a calming song, or two gratitude thoughts.
   - » Tell your brain: *"It's safe to rest."*
2. **Wiggle, Jump, Stretch**
   - » Do something active every day.
   - » Examples: a dance party, a bike ride, a walk around the block, jumping on a trampoline, or playing a sport.
   - » When your body moves, your brain feels braver.
3. **Bravery Bites**
   - » Eat colorful foods to fuel your body.
   - » Add foods that make your brain feel strong, like:

     — turkey and crunchy veggies (B vitamins)

     — fish or walnuts (Omega-3s)

     — bananas or leafy greens (magnesium)

     — yogurt, cheese, eggs, or chicken (amino acids)

     — fortified cereals (vitamin D)
   - » Every brave bite is a win.

4. **Four Square Breathing**

   » Hold up a finger and trace a square in the air or on your knee.

   » Inhale for 4 (draw the first side)

   » Hold for 4 (second side)

   » Exhale for 4 (third side)

   » Hold for 4 (fourth side)

   » Every square you draw helps your brain remember: *I am safe.*

   » Your body works hard for you. Caring for it helps it care for you back.

Parent/Caregiver Practices

1. **Prioritize Your Sleep**
   - » Give yourself the same gentle wind-down you'd offer your child: soft lighting, no screens, a gentle ritual of release.
   - » When your body rests well, your presence becomes calm and steady for your child.
   - » Rest is not a reward for getting everything right. It is a right.
2. **Move with Kindness**
   - » Choose movement that feels grounding: a walk, stretching, or dancing in the kitchen.
   - » Movement helps your body release what your heart holds.
   - » When your body moves, your mind can breathe.
3. **Feed Yourself with Compassion**
   - » Don't skip meals while focusing on theirs. Sit, sip, nourish.
   - » Incorporate lots of whole foods. They will provide the best nutrients.
   - » Your body deserves the same care you advocate for.

4. **Practice a Daily Pause**
    - Take one minute to inhale slowly and exhale fully every time the day feels heavy.
    - Just one minute a day can reset your nervous system.
    - Your breath regulates theirs.

Why it matters . . .

When you nourish your body, your child learns theirs is worth nourishing too.

Your well-being is not separate from your child's healing. It's a powerful part of it.

Health is not perfection—it's alignment.

The moment your mind and body begin working together, healing becomes possible.

As you nourish your body, your strength returns. Your calm returns. **You return.**

Because wholeness isn't something you achieve, **it's something your body remembers.**

4

R—Radical Love: Living with Care, Honesty, and Clear Boundaries

---

"Radical love isn't rescuing—it's remembering that real love trusts growth more than control."

Natalia

Leaving Rogers gave me mixed feelings. Part of me was proud of myself for getting through it, and I was feeling so much better. I was excited to see my friends again and get back in the pool. But I was also scared. I felt out of place at school, and like they didn't know how to handle my return. I received so many stares and questions from other kids that it alone made me want to stay home. At Rogers, I had help all day, people who understood OCD and knew how to talk to it. Once I got home, that help was gone. I was worried my OCD was going to get worse again, like before Rogers.

Then, just a few weeks after coming home, COVID began to spread.

At first, I thought it would be fun with no school, and time at home. I felt almost relieved that some of my biggest worries, school and swimming, were put on pause. But it didn't take long for my brain to latch onto COVID. I wasn't afraid of getting COVID in the beginning, but once I heard that stomach problems were a symptom, I went into fight-or-flight mode. Suddenly, everywhere I turned, people talked about germs, sickness, and hand sanitizer. The lines between real threat and anxiety blurred.

Prior to the lockdown, I would come home from school and wash my hands exactly three times. That was the amount my brain required to remove the germs on my hands, ensuring nothing from school had come home with me. My mom found out I was doing this and would only let me wash my hands once for thirty seconds. I remember feeling a rush of anger because she didn't understand; I *needed* to clean my hands. I couldn't keep those germs on my body. But underneath that anger was relief. Deep down, I knew she was right.

There were a lot of moments like that. Moments when I wanted her to make it stop, to say, "Okay, just this once." But she didn't. She wouldn't. And even though it made me mad, it also made me feel safe. She wasn't afraid of my fear anymore.

When school started again, everything was strange. Now there were masks, social distancing, and half-online days. At first, I liked being home. But when I went back in person, the anxiety hit hard. New teachers, new school, new rules, and new fears of contracting COVID. And then there were grades. Real letter grades, since I was now in middle school.

That's when perfectionism resurfaced. If I didn't get an A, I felt I'd failed. Some days I'd sit at home at my desk, frustrated and crying because I didn't understand something right away. They were angry tears. In elementary school, everything came easily to me. Middle school was harder, and if something didn't click in my brain right away, I would go into panic mode. Mom would come in and say, "If you already knew it, it wouldn't be learning." I hated it when she said that. But it was true.

One time, when my frustration got too big, she said, "I'm going to the living room. I'll come back when I can talk to *you*, not your OCD." I remember being furious. It felt like she was giving up on me. But now I know she was showing me that *I* had a choice too. I could talk back to OCD. I could calm myself down. And I did. It took some time. This happened frequently, but eventually I began to have agency. Now I can usually identify when my OCD has ahold of something, but Mom has always known when I need a reminder.

Mom didn't let me quit piano either, even though I begged her to. I was so angry every time I played. I would get so mad at myself, my mom, my teacher, and at the world because I wasn't perfect. At the time, having to take lessons felt unfair. Now I understand what she was doing. Piano was more than music. It was practice for my OCD. Practice for being uncomfortable, for not being perfect, and for trying again. This was a form of exposure therapy my mom was giving me after Rogers, which helped me distinguish the pursuit of excellence and learn that my perfectionism was really my OCD.

I used to think love meant Mom doing everything to make me feel safe. To cater to my fears.

Radical love isn't always hugs and "yes." Sometimes it's boundaries and "not yet." Now I see that love meant her believing I could handle what scared me. I could defeat OCD. Love meant teaching me how to overcome OCD on my own.

That was the real not giving up on me.

Nanette

On Valentine's Day of 2020, Natalia graduated from Rogers, a fitting day to celebrate love.

I watched her leave the program, proud of all the parts of herself she reclaimed. We were both hopeful, but she was still so delicate.

Just as we were settling into a new normal, the world changed dramatically one month later when everything shut down.

From experience, I knew completing a treatment program isn't the hardest part of recovery. The real work begins afterward. When the scaffolding of support is gone, you have to live the healing you've practiced. Our safety net vanished when a virus closed the world. The germs and the fear felt real again, but with a new name—COVID-19.

This sudden isolation tested Natalia's coping skills and confronted her with a new kind of fear.

At home together daily, OCD lingered as the pandemic continued, giving Natalia's old fears new context. Her worries about illness quieted, but never disappeared.

Every so often, she asked to check her temperature. Each time, her eyes would find mine. Before Rogers, I would have given in to the silent pleas, the old patterns stirring, wanting to soothe her fear with comfort. But I'd witnessed what that surrender cost her. With every act of reassurance, OCD crept in. Love ached to comfort. Fear demanded control.

So instead, I'd gently say, "That would be feeding your anxiety. How about we sit with the feeling until it goes down?" Together, we practiced waiting. Breathing. Remembering.

Years of working with children taught me that when you try to extinguish a behavior, it can sometimes flare up before fading. Natalia's OCD brain did just that. It pushed back. But I had changed too. I was learning to respond in new ways. I held compassion *and* boundaries.

This act of holding steady, refusing to feed the OCD, became the essence of radical love: standing firm for true healing. As our journey evolved, shifting from daily struggles to new school challenges, I found that maintaining boundaries was central along every step.

Love, like the brain, is malleable. It stretches. It adapts. It learns new patterns if we let it. The truest love teaches self-trust rather than seeking control or rescue.

That fall, Natalia started middle school. Classes were a hybrid of online and in-person instruction. In hindsight, it was the perfect transition, taking smaller steps and lessening the overwhelm. But middle school brought a new challenge: grades.

OCD is clever. It changes. As worries about germs eased, perfectionism took on a new stage. Natalia grew preoccupied with earning A's, and her frustration mounted when things didn't come easily during home learning. I'd remind her that it's not learning if you already know it.

But her OCD brain didn't like that. Some days, disengaging from her pain tore at me. It felt brutal, almost like abandonment. Even cold. But this was devotion in its rawest form. I didn't step back because I stopped caring: I drew the line because love demanded that I hold steady, refusing fear to take the driver's seat.

I learned to choose when to engage, when to step back, and when to model calm. I often reminded Natalia, "You didn't ask for OCD, but you have it. And because you have it, you have a responsibility to manage it."

Setting boundaries and holding high expectations isn't the absence of love. It is radical love. It means choosing to believe in strength over struggle.

When Natalia asked to quit piano, I told her she could once she finished middle school. I knew that rule sounded firm, but music had become a form of medicine for her brain. Piano was more than practice; it was exposure. Every wrong note was a lesson in imperfection. Every scale was an act of courage.

Radical love doesn't always look soft. Sometimes it looks like saying no with a full heart. It's compassion with a backbone. Love that's strong enough to stay steady through discomfort, because you know that freedom is on the other side.

Love took on a new shape for both of us during that time, connecting everything that came before and leading to the lessons we carry now.

For me, it meant learning to let go of control and remembering that the road to recovery isn't a straight path.

For Natalia, it meant learning that being loved didn't mean being rescued.

What This Means for You

Radical love means caring deeply while setting clear boundaries. It is both gentle and firm. It stays present through discomfort, holding space for growth, and trusting others to handle hard things.

When we love like this, we stop shielding children from discomfort and start helping them build resilience. We show that safety comes not from them avoiding fear, but from learning they can face it and endure.

Radical love uses two hands: One offers comfort, the other upholds boundaries that help growth. Radical love offers the balance of compassion and accountability. It's believing in a child's strength while modeling your own.

Youth Practices

1. **The Choice Voice**
   - When OCD or anxiety get loud, ask yourself: *"Is this my voice, or fear's voice?"*
   - Practice choosing your calm, brave voice instead.
2. **The Not Yet Rule**
   - When you can't do something *right now*, add "yet."
   - Saying, *"I can't do this . . . yet."* reminds your brain that growth is coming.
3. **Radical Self-Talk**
   - When you make a mistake, say, *"I'm learning."*
   - Radical love toward yourself means you don't need to be perfect to be worthy.
4. **Love in Action**
   - Each night, name one time you loved yourself bravely by saying no, trying again, or calming your thoughts.
   - That's radical love in practice.

Parent/Caregiver Practices

1. **Respond, Don't Rescue**
   » Before stepping in, pause and ask yourself: *"Is this comfort, or is this control?"*
   » Offer presence instead of reassurance.
   » Example: *"I'm here with you"* is often the most healing thing you can say.

2. **Set Boundaries with Compassion**
   » Set limits on what your child may do, as well as what you will do for your child.
   » Boundaries aren't walls. They are bridges of trust.
   » Boundaries show your child that love is steady and dependable, not conditional on calm or compliance.

3. **Model Emotional Regulation**
   » When your child's fear rises, show them what grounded looks like by regulating yourself first.
   » Ask questions instead of confronting.
   » Example: *"Is this you talking or your anxiety talking?"*
   » Your inquiry will cultivate their self-awareness.

4. **Hold High Expectations with Heart**
    - Let your child know: *"I believe in you enough to expect your best."*
    - High expectations paired with grace create accountability rooted in love, not pressure.

Radical love doesn't rescue. It remembers. It remembers that love isn't fragile. It remembers that boundaries are a form of care. And it remembers that when love stands steady, everyone learns to stand taller.

5

I —Invest: Healing Isolation Through Connection and Contribution

"Investing in others isn't self-sacrifice—it's remembering that we are needed and we belong."

Natalia

Volunteering was one of the first things that made me feel like *me* again.

At Feed My Starving Children, everyone knew me and said hello when I walked in. They trusted me to help on the warehouse crew, despite my youth. I finally felt like I belonged somewhere outside of my anxiety.

When I was in the fourth grade, I gave a persuasive speech on the importance of volunteering. I had no idea at the time how much those words would matter later. I just knew that helping others made me feel good—grounded, connected, and useful.

Returning to school after Rogers was challenging. I felt different, like people were watching me, trying to figure out what had happened while I was gone. Each day, I wanted to retreat further into myself. But volunteering brought me back into the world. It gave me purpose beyond my noisy, anxious thoughts, and for a moment, I felt seen for something good.

I started volunteering in my dad's kindergarten classroom when I was nine, around the time my OCD had taken over almost every part of my life. Stepping into that classroom made the worries fade. I was needed there. I mattered.

One morning, I read a story to the class like I usually did. Then I went from table to table, helping the kids write their ABC's. I always spent extra time with the quieter students, the ones who seemed to want to disappear. I knew what that felt like.

At the end of the day, the students rushed to hug me like they always did. But that day, the quietest student was the first to reach me. He was smiling, excited. That moment stayed with me. We didn't need to share our stories out loud. We recognized each other. We understood what it felt like to move through the world carrying something invisible.

I used to think I had to be fully healed before I helped anyone. Now I understand something different.

Helping others is part of how I heal.

Every time I share my story, I reclaim another piece of myself. My voice grows braver, one word at a time.

Every time I encourage someone else, I encourage the younger version of me.

Service reminds me that I am not defined by OCD. I am defined by how I love, give, and connect with others.

Service helped me remember that I belong.

Nanette

As a parent, I wanted Natalia to cherish the value of service. When she was five, we began volunteering together at Feed My Starving Children. Side by side at long tables, we scooped rice and soy into small bags for children we would never meet. Those moments were simple, but profound.

The shift leaders knew her by name. They noticed her effort. Later, they trusted her to work on the warehouse crew. She wasn't seen as "the anxious child" or "the kid with OCD." She was simply part of the team, and that mattered.

After her diagnosis, I came to understand how deeply mental illness isolates. Fear can make the world feel smaller. Silence grows heavy. Even a single moment of connection lets your world breathe again.

Service became more than helping others. It helped Natalia stay rooted in herself. Through it, she remembered her worth, felt capable, and rebuilt an identity beyond fear. She was needed, and she knew it.

Over time, service grew into advocacy. Natalia began sharing her story so other kids wouldn't feel as alone as she once had.

In early 2024, she was invited to co-emcee a major mental health fundraising event. As the lights came up, I didn't see the child who once couldn't sleep alone. I saw a young woman speaking with steadiness and courage—not because fear was gone, but because it no longer defined her.

That night, I realized she hadn't become someone new. She had simply come home to herself.

Service didn't just help her heal. It reignited her sense of belonging—the quiet, steady knowing that she mattered, even with fear still present.

Connection rebuilds what fear undermines. Contribution expands the world again.

You don't have to be "better" to offer something meaningful. Willingness is enough.

What This Means for You

Isolation whispers, *You are alone.*

Connection gently answers, *You belong.*

Connection is critical to healing.

Giving does not require perfection. It doesn't require confidence or having everything figured out. It only requires **showing up**.

Each act of service expands our world, strengthens identity, rebuilds hope, and connects us beyond our struggles.

When we invest in others, we don't lose ourselves. We rediscover who we are. Service restores a sense of belonging, identity, and hope.

Youth Practices

1. **The Kindness Countdown**

   » Do one small act of kindness each day.

   » Examples:

   — Compliment someone.

   — Share a snack.

   — Text a friend.

   » Notice how it makes *you* feel.

2. **Helping Hand Jar**

   » Gather an empty jar.

   » Add a bead, stone, or note each time you help someone.

   » Watch your kindness grow.

3. **The Noticing Game**

   » When you feel overwhelmed, look for one good thing happening in the room.

   » Look for one place where you could offer kindness.

   » This gently shifts your brain from fear to connection.

4. **You Matter Moment**
    - Each night, say or journal one way you made someone's day easier or better.
    - Even tiny actions matter for building confidence and connection.
    - This reminds your brain, "I matter. I am part of something."

Parent/Caregiver Practices

1. **The Light List**
   - » Together, list the people, places, and causes that spark warmth, curiosity, or care.
   - » These are the places where connection can grow.
   - » Add to the list over time. As it grows, it will reflect your family values, not your fears.
2. **Serve Side by Side**
   - » Choose one shared act of service.
   - » Examples:
     - — Packing lunches for a community pantry
     - — Reading to shelter animals
     - — Making and sending cards to nursing homes
   - » Healing grows through shared meaning.
3. **Microconnection Moments**
   - » Connection does not require grand gestures.
   - » Examples:
     - — Wave to a neighbor.
     - — Smile at a cashier.
     - — Hold the door open for someone.
   - » These tiny reconnections soften isolation.

4. **Notice Their Impact**
   - Notice small acts of connection and their impact.
   - Example: "I saw how gently you helped him. That mattered."
   - This builds identity from the inside out.

We heal through connection.

We grow through community.

We remember ourselves by belonging.

Connection doesn't erase struggle, but it makes us strong enough to move through it.

You were never meant to heal alone.

And you don't have to.

6

V—Vulnerability: Releasing Guilt and Shame Through Forgiveness

---

"Forgiveness isn't forgetting—it's remembering who we are beneath the shame."

Natalia

I wanted so badly to be like other kids, to do the things they did without thinking twice. Around third and fourth grade, birthday sleepovers were the big thing. Everyone was doing them. And I wanted to try.

For years, I went to the parties, laughed, played the games, and ate the cake. But then my mom would have to come pick me up before bedtime. One October, I decided to try staying the whole night. I knew the family well. I trusted them. I felt ready to face this new challenge.

We lined up our sleeping bags in the basement. Everyone fell asleep except me. As the room got quieter, the noise in my mind got louder.

What if I get sick?

What if I panic?

What if I can't get to Mom?

My brain spiraled. The panic hit hard. I ran upstairs to the bathroom, hands shaking. I couldn't get sick in someone else's house. I couldn't. I tried to push through. I tried my breathing techniques and my audiobooks, but nothing was helping with the racing, panicking thoughts I was having.

At four a.m., I finally called my mom.

She picked up on the first ring.

Twenty minutes later, she pulled into the driveway. I slipped quietly out the back deck door so I wouldn't wake anyone. Mom held me through the panic. My breathing eventually slowed, and I told her I wanted to try again.

She turned the car around without hesitation.

When I crept back inside, I accidentally woke my friend's dad. He saw me wandering at dawn and probably wondered what I was doing. I felt humiliated and too embarrassed to share the truth. I didn't know how to explain why my mom had driven there twice. Ashamed, I couldn't admit that anxiety had won again.

For years, I beat myself up about that night.

But now, looking back, I see it differently.

I see a girl who tried.

I see a mom who came.

I see courage, not failure.

Forgiveness doesn't always look like letting go.

Sometimes it looks like letting ourselves be human.

Nanette

As a mother, even after an entire career in education, I was unprepared for parenting a child with OCD. There is no class, workshop, or degree that teaches how to navigate the fear deeply rooted in your child's mind. Because Natalia's symptoms were complex and mostly invisible, my feelings of inadequacy were sharper and heavier. I felt as if I was failing at the most important job of my life.

When Natalia was in fourth grade and still seeing her psychologist weekly, we were nearing her December birthday. I wished for just one year, one moment, when she could enjoy her birthday free from overwhelming fear. I had tried herbal supplements in the past, but they hadn't helped. Desperation pressed in. I wanted relief for her, and for us.

After talking with Natalia's psychologist and pediatrician, we decided to try the smallest dose of Prozac—5 mg. It felt like the cautious, responsible thing to do.

At the same time, we were invited to Florida to spend winter break with close friends. Natalia loved Harry Potter, so her birthday present was a visit to The Wizarding World of Harry Potter. She had read every book and memorized every spell. I hoped this trip would bring us the magic I longed for.

But as we spent more days by the ocean, something shifted. Her behaviors weren't just anxious; they were unfamiliar. Warped. When we returned home, Natalia told me, through tears and trembling breaths, that she was having frightening new thoughts.

Thoughts about harming herself.

Thoughts she had never had before.

Thoughts that were not hers.

My world collapsed in an instant.

We soon learned that Natalia was in the 3 percent of children who metabolize antidepressants too quickly, a group more vulnerable to suicide ideation.

We stopped the medication immediately. The thoughts eventually faded.

But the guilt did not. It clung to me like wet sand—heavy, sticky, impossible to shake off, no matter how hard I tried. I replayed my decision a thousand times.

Why did I doubt my intuition?

Why did I make the wrong choice?

Why did I let something hurt her so deeply?

Instead of helping, I had unintentionally made everything worse.

I carried that guilt into every appointment, every bedtime, every moment of fear. It wrapped itself around my heart until I felt unworthy of being her mother.

I punished myself daily. Quietly. Brutally.

I prayed the thoughts would never return.

I feared what my choice had done to her brain, her trust, and her future.

It wasn't until we arrived at Rogers, a year later, that I finally felt Natalia was safe enough and I could start facing my guilt honestly.

And when I did, my healing began.

I had heard about mirror work and started trying it. I looked in the mirror every morning and whispered to myself: *"I forgive you."*

It felt awkward at first. Some days, I believed it. And some days, I didn't.

But sticking with it became a doorway back to myself.

Forgiveness didn't erase the pain. But it allowed me to remember who I was beneath the guilt, a mother doing her very best through unimaginable circumstances.

And that, I learned, is vulnerability.

Not confession.

Not collapse.

But choosing honesty over self-punishment, and compassion over blame.

What This Means for You

Vulnerability is not collapsing, it's opening.

It's the moment we stop pretending we have it all together and start letting truth lead.

When we meet our mistakes with compassion instead of punishment, guilt and shame loosen their grips. When we tell the truth without hiding, we teach our children to do the same.

Forgiveness doesn't rewrite the past.

It rewrites how the past lives within us.

And vulnerability is the doorway to remembering who we are beneath the fear.

Youth Practices

1. **Safe Voice vs. Fear Voice**
   - Ask: *"Is this my real voice, or fear's voice?"*
   - This helps us separate our identity from intrusive thoughts.
2. **Heart-Hand Breathing**
   - Hand on heart, hand on belly.
   - Slow inhale: *"I'm learning."*
   - Exhale: *"I'm safe."*
3. **The Shame Reframe**
   - Write a letter to your younger self about an experience that embarrassed, humiliated, or shamed you.
   - Reframing turns shame into compassion.
4. **Kindness Catcher**
   - Each night, write one way you were kind to yourself:
   - Took a break.
   - Said "not yet."
   - Named a fear.
   - Asked for help.

These moments build self-forgiveness.

Parent/Caregiver Practices

1. **Mirror Forgiveness Ritual**
   - Look at yourself with softness—even for five seconds.
   - Say: *"I forgive you. You were doing the best you could."*
2. **Name the Guilt**
   - Write down the guilt you carry.
   - Underneath, write what you know now that you didn't know then.
   - Watch the shame lose its power.
3. **Repair Out Loud**
   - Narrate your mistakes with gentleness.
   - Model emotional courage, not perfection.
   - Example: *"I shouldn't have said that. Let's try again."*
4. **The BS Jar (Blame/Shame)**
   - Each time you catch yourself in blame or shame, add a coin or dollar to the jar.
   - Use it to fund a small family joy: ice cream, a movie, a hike.

Forgiveness doesn't free us from our past—it frees us *to return* to who we've been all along.

When we practice vulnerability with ourselves, our children learn courage through us.

And when guilt and shame lift, even a little, our wholeness comes back into view.

7

E—Explore: Discovering Interests, Strengths, and Joy

"Exploration is the courage to try, not knowing who you'll be—and trusting you'll meet yourself there."

Natalia

Performance anxiety showed up early in my life, especially at piano recitals. I hated being on stage. It took so much energy just to get through a performance that I never actually enjoyed it. My body would tense, my thoughts would race, and I just wanted it to be over.

That's why my mom was so surprised when I told her I wanted to try a pageant.

Honestly, I didn't really know what a pageant was or what it involved. I just saw the wardrobe and the sparkle, and something inside me lit up. For the first time in a long time, I felt curious instead of afraid.

Our family friends connected us with a coach, and soon I was signed up to participate in a pageant that summer. Through the process, I learned so much more than how to walk or pose. My coach helped me develop my personal platform advocating for mental health, which mattered deeply to me. As I practiced speaking about my story, I began to realize that my experiences didn't make me weak—they gave me a voice.

Pageants aren't just about appearance. They're about discovering who you are, what you care about, and how you show up in the world. And through this experience, I learned a lot about who I want to be—and what makes me, me.

I was definitely nervous going into the pageant. Not because I didn't believe in myself, but because this was new, and new things used to give my anxiety a lot of power. I competed in several optional events, including modeling, which helped me gain confidence on stage. The spokesmodel and talent were the most nerve-racking, but I managed my anxiety and stayed present. After each one, I felt proud—not because I was perfect, but because I showed up.

By the time the required competitions were over, I already knew something important: No matter the outcome, I was glad I had tried. I had fun. I made friends. I stood on stage multiple times in front of an audience, and I was okay.

And then something unexpected happened. I won.

But the real win wasn't the title. It was discovering that anxiety didn't get to decide what I tried anymore. It was realizing that I could feel fear and still move forward.

That weekend, I didn't just compete. I discovered a part of myself I hadn't seen before.

And that changed everything.

Nanette

As a former dance line captain and NFL professional cheerleader, many people assumed my daughter would follow the same path. I tried enrolling Natalia in tap and ballet at age three, but she quickly made it clear—it wasn't her thing. I didn't push it. Years of weigh-ins and body scrutiny had deeply shaped my own relationship with movement and food, fueling an eating disorder I carried for far too long. I didn't want that for her.

Instead, I introduced Natalia to a variety of activities—skating with hockey skates, softball, soccer. She tried them all for a while. Swimming became her favorite, until OCD eventually found its way there too.

By late 2020, I had no idea a new interest was quietly waiting to be discovered.

Over the holidays, we were visiting friends when Natalia went upstairs with their daughter, a former Miss Minnesota Teen USA. When she came back down, her eyes were bright in a way I hadn't seen for a long time. She talked about the crown, the gowns, the heels—the glam of it all. Then she said, simply, "I would like to try a pageant."

My mind raced. I knew the stereotypes. I also knew pageants could be something much more: public speaking, leadership, service, confidence, and self-discovery. With OCD in the picture, it felt like it could either support her healing or threaten it.

At the same time, OCD had already taken so much of her childhood. I wanted her to have something to look forward to. I also deeply believed that my role as a parent wasn't to choose her passions, but to expose her to possibilities and let *her* discover what fit. I had seen too many children pushed into activities that served adult expectations rather than their own joy.

With careful consideration, age-appropriate guidance, and the support of people who understood the industry, I said yes.

Eight months later, we stood together in a dressing room. Natalia had just finished the opening number and was changing into her formal gown. I hugged her and told her how proud I was. Tears welled up. Not from nerves, but from awe: Awe at all she had already survived. Awe at her willingness to try something uncertain. Awe at her ability to remain whole, even with OCD along for the ride.

She looked at me—steady, confident—and said, "No. Don't cry yet. You only get to cry when I win this thing. And I'm about to go do that right now."

Watching Natalia step onto that stage, I realized something essential: Exploration is not about the activity itself. It's about what happens *inside* a child when fear loosens its grip and curiosity is allowed to lead.

For years, anxiety had narrowed her world. Now, she was expanding it, and on her own terms.

This is what exploration makes possible.

What This Means for You

Exploration is not about finding the "right" activity or achieving a specific outcome. It's about reopening doors that fear has quietly closed.

For children living with anxiety or mental illness, fear often convinces them that safety comes from avoidance. But exploration gently teaches a different truth: that discomfort is not danger, and curiosity can exist alongside fear.

When children are given permission to explore—without pressure, comparison, or expectation—they begin to trust themselves again. Confidence doesn't come from winning or excelling; it comes from trying, learning, and discovering that they can handle what they once avoided.

As parents, our role is not to decide who our children should become. It's to create space where they are free to discover who they already are. When we replace control with curiosity, we offer them a powerful message:

You are allowed to explore.

You are allowed to change.

You are allowed to become.

Youth Practices

1. **The Try-It List**
   - Write down three things you're curious about—big or small.
   - Choose one to try this month, just for fun.
   - You don't have to be good at it. Trying counts.

2. **Brave Beginnings**
   - Before trying something new, say: *"I don't have to be perfect. I just have to begin."*
   - Beginning is how confidence grows.

3. **Joy Check-In**
   - After an activity, ask yourself:

     — *"Did this give me energy or take it away?"*

     — *"Did I feel more like myself?"*
   - Let your answers guide what you explore next.

4. **Permission Slips**
   - Write yourself a note that says:

     — *"I give myself permission to try new things—and to change my mind."*
   - Keep the note somewhere you can see it.

Parent/Caregiver Practices

1. **Offer Exposure, Not Expectation**
   - » Introduce your child to activities without attaching outcomes.
   - » Say: "Let's try it and see how it feels," instead of "Let's see how good you are."
   - » Curiosity builds confidence; pressure shuts it down.
2. **Let Joy Be the Measure**
   - » Notice what energizes your child rather than drains them.
   - » Reflect it back: *"I noticed how alive you seemed doing that."*
   - » Joy is often the most honest guide.
3. **Separate Worth from Performance**
   - » Praise effort, courage, and willingness—regardless of results.
   - » Example: *"I'm proud of you for trying something new."*
   - » This creates safety in exploration.

4. **Engage in Your Own Passions**
    - Explore your own hobbies and passions.
    - This shows that we all have different interests and strengths.
    - Share why you enjoy this activity. This models self-care and worthiness.

Exploration isn't about finding the final version of yourself. It's about staying open to who you are becoming.

And when curiosity is allowed to lead, confidence follows—not all at once, but steadily, honestly, and in ways that last.

8

Living the THHRIVE Path

Healing did not arrive all at once for us. It unfolded slowly, unevenly, and often in circles.

There were moments of clarity followed by setbacks. Seasons of hope interrupted by fear. Times when we felt grounded and steady, and others when we found ourselves revisiting familiar struggles—this time with more awareness, but no less tenderness. What we learned, over time, is that healing is not a destination to reach or a problem to solve.

It is a way of living.

The THHRIVE path is not something you complete. It is something you return to.

Again and again.

We began by remembering what had always been true: that we were not broken. That beneath diagnosis, behavior, fear, and exhaustion, wholeness was already present. This remembering did not erase the hard parts—it simply stopped them from defining us.

From there, we learned how to ask for help. Not as a last resort, but as an act of wisdom. We learned to reach beyond ourselves without shame, and to accept support as part of being human. Help did not make us weaker; it made us more honest.

Caring for the body taught us that healing is not only emotional or intellectual. Sleep, nourishment, movement, and breath became messages of safety to a nervous system that lived too long in survival mode. As the body softened, the mind followed—not perfectly, but enough to feel possibility again.

Love asked more of us than comfort. It required boundaries. Steadiness. The courage to believe in growth rather than control. We learned that true love does not rescue—it trusts. It stays present when fear demands relief. It holds firm when old patterns try to return.

Connection became medicine. Investing in others—through service, contribution, and belonging—healed isolation in ways nothing else could. Giving outwardly restored something inward, reminding us that purpose grows when we are part of something larger than our pain.

Vulnerability opened the door to forgiveness. Guilt and shame loosened their grip when they were brought into the light. We learned that forgiveness is not forgetting. It is remembering who we are beneath blame, fear, and regret.

And then, we returned to life itself.

Exploration did not erase fear, but it expanded possibility. Curiosity reopened doors anxiety had quietly closed. Confidence grew not from achievement, but from trying—discovering joy, agency, and voice along the way.

I still live with OCD. And that has never been the measure of my wholeness.

This journey was never about removing parts of me (or my mom) that felt inconvenient, frightening, or misunderstood. Healing was not the absence of anxiety, nor the elimination of struggle. It was an invitation to relate differently to every part of ourselves.

To stop fighting what was present. To listen instead of resist. To understand how even the hardest parts were trying, in their own way, to protect.

Healing became an act of integration.

An embracing of the whole self—strength and fear, courage and doubt, joy and grief. Nothing needed to be erased for wholeness to exist. Wholeness was already there, waiting to be remembered.

This is the THHRIVE path.

Not linear. Not perfect. Not finished.

It is a rhythm. A way of meeting life with honesty, compassion, courage, and trust. Some days you may stand firmly in one principle; other days you may circle back to another. Both belong.

Healing does not promise a life without challenge. It offers a life with meaning.

And when we walk this path with grace, toward ourselves and one another, we don't become someone new.

We remember who we have always been, and learn to see it clearly at last.

What follows is not instruction. It is relationship.

Two voices. Two perspectives. One shared path.

This is where the framework becomes love.

Epilogue

Some stories can only be told together.

What follows is not a conclusion, but a reflection—two voices shaped by the same journey, seeing it from different sides.

This is what the THHRIVE path looks like when it is lived, not explained.

Dear Mom,

When I was younger, I thought love meant making the fear stop. I thought love meant fixing it—relieving my OCD, taking it away, saying yes when everything felt too big. And when you didn't, I sometimes thought it meant you didn't understand.

Now I know you understood more than I did.

You weren't trying to make my life harder. You were trying to help me defeat my OCD. You knew I could do it. You saw strength in me before I could see it in myself. When you didn't give in, it didn't mean you weren't listening. It meant you believed I could handle what scared me.

There were moments that felt unfair. Moments when I was angry. Moments when I thought you didn't understand what was wrong with me, or that you were being too hard. But now I see that you were steady when everything else felt shaky. You helped me learn that I could face OCD on my own. Even during the fights, you helped me notice when OCD was taking over. Because of that, I can now recognize what I need—and when OCD is creeping back in.

I know myself now in a way I couldn't have imagined back then. I know I am capable. I know I am strong. I know that anxiety doesn't get to decide what I try or who I become. You gave me the skills I needed to move from the darkness of struggling into the light of awareness and hope.

Thank you for staying. Thank you for holding boundaries. Thank you for loving me in a way that helped me grow.

Because of you, I know I can face hard things.

Love,

Natalia

Dear Natalia,

This month you turned seventeen—ten years after you were formally diagnosed with OCD. Some parents wish time would stand still, that moments could be frozen and held forever. I am not one of them. I have watched time move us forward, sometimes painfully, sometimes gently, always shaping us.

I stood by as OCD took hold of so many parts of your life. I watched it shrink your world, steal ease, and demand more than any child should have to give. But I also witnessed something far more powerful. I watched you remember who you are—and reclaim your life.

That has been the most meaningful part of this journey.

So many memories blur together from those years, lost in the effort of simply surviving and doing the next right thing. But if I were given the choice to go back and change any part of it, I wouldn't. Not a single moment. Because I have seen who you have become beyond OCD, and that is something any mother would be endlessly proud of.

You are kind. Honest. Thoughtful. Funny. Compassionate. Insightful. Strong. You are deeply self-aware, and you have developed coping skills and emotional wisdom that many adults spend a lifetime trying to learn. You meet yourself with honesty and courage, even when it's hard.

Years ago, when your younger self asked me why this was happening, I didn't have an answer I could stand on. I offered what I could, but I wasn't certain. Now I am.

You have come to understand that pain is not an enemy to defeat, but a teacher to listen to. You have learned acceptance instead of resistance, and in doing so, you have taught me more than I ever imagined possible. We have both been changed by this path.

Walking alongside you through this journey has been the greatest privilege of my life.

Thank you for trusting me.

Thank you for choosing me.

And thank you for becoming exactly who you are.

Love,

Mom

And this is how healing happened:
not by fixing what was broken,
but by learning to see ourselves clearly,
through her eyes.

Acknowledgments

This book was shaped by many people, moments, and acts of quiet support.

We are deeply grateful to our family, friends, teachers, therapists, coaches, and care teams who walked alongside us through seasons of fear, hope, and healing. Thank you to those who believed in us when the path felt uncertain, who held space without trying to fix, and who reminded us—again and again—that wholeness was always present.

We are especially thankful to the individuals who offered their time, care, and honest presence during the creation of this book, including:

» *Grandma*

» *Our beta readers*

» *The PrairieCare and Rogers Behavioral Health teams*

» *Educators, mentors, and advocates who supported this journey*

And to every family navigating anxiety, OCD, or mental illness: thank you for your courage, your honesty, and your willingness to stay. This book exists because of you.

About the Authors

Natalia Yurecko is a mental health advocate, speaker, and student who uses her lived experience with OCD and anxiety to support youth and families navigating mental health challenges. She is a grassroots advocate with the International OCD Foundation, where she works to raise awareness, reduce stigma, and amplify youth voices. Through storytelling, advocacy, and service, Natalia reminds others that they are not broken and that healing is possible without erasing who they are. She speaks to educators, legislators, and community audiences, using her platform to promote compassion, understanding, and access to mental health support.

Nanette Yurecko is a retired educator, best-selling co-author, and family advocate with a career dedicated to supporting children and families navigating emotional and behavioral challenges. She is a certified family support group facilitator with the National Alliance on Mental Illness (NAMI), where she supports caregivers through education, connection, and shared lived experience. Drawing from both professional leadership and lived parenting, Nanette brings a perspective grounded in compassion, resilience, and truth, helping families move from survival into meaningful, connected lives.

Together, Natalia and Nanette share a story shaped by honesty, courage, and love—offering a perspective that bridges generations and reminds readers that healing is not about fixing what is broken, but remembering what has always been whole.

www.ingramcontent.com/pod-product-compliance
Lightning Source LLC
LaVergne TN
LVHW090534110826
845146LV00003B/1085

* 9 7 9 8 9 9 5 0 5 4 0 0 9 *